"Take a road-trip away in your old split screen, or picture a baywindow in the same scene, choose a route to unknown places, taste new flavours and meet new and old faces"

CONTENTS

© 2010 Fan Of The Van™ and Origocom Repro AB. All rights reserved. Unauthorized copying is prohibited.
Photo by Lelle Hannu and Steve Rooker. Some pictures are taken by bus-owners with kind permission for
VW Camper Cookbook to use in this book. Some pictures have been given to us without any information of
source and are published with the best of intentions and in good trust. The crew of *VW Camper Cookbook*
apologises for any unintentional errors or omissions which will be corrected in future editions of this book.
Creative Directors: Lennart Hannu/Origocom Repro and Steve Rooker/Fan Of The Van™. Typefont used: Bliss.
VW Camper Cookbook is printed in the E.U. by Tallinna Raamatutrükikoja OÜ, Estonia. Paper: 150 gr Arctic Silk.
Third print/5.000 copies. • www.vwcampercookbook.com • www.fanofthevan.com • www.origorepro.com
ISBN 978-91-631-9684-3   *Also available in Germany as "Das Original VW Bulli Kochbuch"*

Steve Rooker   Susanne Rooker   Lennart Hannu

THE ORIGINAL
VW CAMPER COOKBOOK

VW Van fans!

The time has come to drive past the drive thru! Find that cool place and get gastronomic in the great outdoors. Contained within the pages of this VW cookbook is the ultimate guide to campervan style cooking with safety tips, storage solutions and what essential equipment to have. It doesn't matter what type of VW you drive, a ratty split panel or a show winning samba, there is nothing stopping you from cooking up a storm with our tailor-made, easy and inspirational camping recipes.

Enjoy the freedom your van gives you with friends and family. Kickback, take it easy and have fun!

Just drive on by...

Campervan safety and storage

SAFETY FIRST

Before attempting any cooking in the great outdoors in your treasured campervan think safety. Prepare your van so you can deal with accidents that could arise.

Fire is the one we all dread, the last thing you want to see is your precious campervan disappear in flames and this can happen incredibly fast. So having a good fire extinguisher is a must have item. Don't leave home without one and keep it somewhere that is easily accessible. Fire blankets are also a good cheap extra insurance that pack up small.

Another essential item before heading out on the highway is a good well stocked first aid kit. Also check your gas hoses from the bottle to the stove. They get old and can crack and perish.

Lastly, don't forget to check you have enough gas for your trip!

ZIP LOCK BAGS
Great for keeping dry goods such as rice and pasta and for marinating meat. They fill the gaps in fridges and cupboards more efficiently than original packets and plastic containers.

PLASTIC CONTAINERS WITH LIDS
Certain ingredients will squash in ziplock bags, then you need a hard container.

MINIATURE BOTTLES
These small bottles are great for keeping oils, dressings and sauces in. You can find all kinds of sizes to suit all your needs.

Essential cooking equipment

KITCHEN KNIFE
There is a knife made by victorinox. It is the ultimate all-round kitchen knife. Buy one of these versatile knives, as it is all you will need.

PLASTIC CHOPPING BOARD – Don't think a small one is a good idea, it's not. It will be frustrating to use. Choose one with a good usable size. They are thin and light and pack away easily.

UTENSILS
Whisk, ladel, tongs, spoons and can opener.

PANS – Normally you have only a couple of gas rings in the average campervan, so there is really no reason to have more than three pans. One frying-pan and two sauce-pans with lids. If you buy non-stick, keep your kitchen cloths in-between when packed so you don't ruin the coatings.

PLASTIC BOWL
Useful for whipping cream, mixing salads and at the end of the day washing-up.

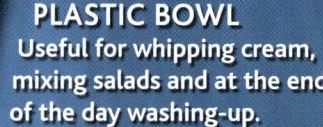

TIN FOIL PACK

METAL OR WOODEN SKEWERS

Do not take up much room, great for bbq meat and veggies. If you pre-soak the wooden scewers in water for an hour they won't burn on the grill.

BARBEQUES

Many opt for the disposable type of barbeque. They are very cheap, easy to light and can be purchased on route. However, there are better options such as the drum, bucket and fold flat barbeques. These are all better but by far the best are the dome lid type.

Cleaning a barbeque can be a chore. Make life easier, take a plastic bag big enough for your barbeque and once cool seal it in the bag and clean it when you come home.

WATER CARRIERS

The collapsible types are the best suited for campervans. They store flat and take up little room.

WASHING-UP LIQUID

Decanter some washing-up liquid from home into a smaller bottle just enough for your trip. Don't take the whole bottle from home. It will just take up too much space.

WASHING-UP SPONGE

Scourers are favourable over brushes as again they pack down smaller. Think about making the washing-up easier by filling the dirty pans with water and wash-ing-up liquid directly after you have used them. The remaining heat in the pan and in the stove helps the washing-up liquid break it down.

Soups and salads

Sunny hazy days, cruising to the beach, sitting in the shade or catching some rays and eating outside a tasty summer salad. Or when you find yourself in the van and outside it's raining cats and dogs, it's a good time to make a hot bowl of soup, listen to the radio, maybe open a book or park up on a headland and watch the waves roll in.

Avocado salad

INGREDIENTS (2 portions)

3 rashers of smoked bacon or pancetta
1 cooked chicken breast
1 tbsp of olive oil
Mixed salad leaves
2 ripe avocados, halved and
the stones removed

DRESSING (2 portions)

6 tbsp extra virgin olive oil
1 tbsp cider vinegar
1 clove of garlic, crushed
1 tsp Dijon mustard
Salt and pepper

Tip: How to choose ripe avocados!
-Don't push your thumb into them, instead
squeeze them slightly in the palm of your hand.
If the avocado gives a little, then it's ripe.

METHOD
Fry the bacon/pancetta in the oil until very
crispy. Tear the cooked chicken breast into
small pieces. With the salad leaves in a bowl,
slice pieces of the avocado into the leaves,
add the bacon and chicken.

To make the dressing:
Place all the ingredients into a bowl. Use a
fork or small whisk and beat the ingredients
together. This can be prepared at home and
poured into a miniature bottle.
   Toss the salad in the dressing just before
serving.

Rikki James drives this 1954 Barndoor samba hard! And so would you if you had a 2.6 ltr 914 Porsche engine with a 911 5 speed Porsche box! This bus was the first to do a sub 18 second pass for the BWA! Check out www.buseswithattitude.co.uk

Greek salad

Utensils

Bowl

INGREDIENTS (2 portions)

Mixed leaves
½ red onion
Tomatoes
1 green pepper
100 g feta cheese
Black olives (Kalamata olives are the best!)

(Dressing: page 134)

METHOD
Slice the onion into rings. Cube the feta cheese and cut the green pepper into small triangle pieces. Mix all the ingredients together and drizzle over the seasoned oil.

Darren Wilsons' 1964 13 window Italian splitty.

VOLKSWAGEN

Caesar salad

INGREDIENTS (2 portions)

1 chicken breast
Mixed leaves
Parmesan
Croutons

DRESSING

1 cup mayonnaise
1 tbsp lemon juice
1 tbsp worcestershire sauce
1 clove of crushed garlic
Salt and pepper
2 tbsp grated parmesan cheese
Dash of milk

METHOD
Make the dressing by mixing all the ingredients together. Fry or grill the chicken. Slice the chicken into bite-size pieces. Place the mixed leaves in a bowl. Add shavings of parmesan, croutons and chicken. Add dressing to taste and toss the ingredients around in the bowl. Serve with fresh bread.

CAMPMOBILE
WESTFALIA

Jeff Ashman's 1977 Westfalia Berlin.

Lentil soup

Håkan Nordin from Stockholm is regullary seen cruising the roads of Sweden in his 1965 21 window Samba.

INGREDIENTS (2 portions)

½ cup (100 ml) dried red or green lentils
2 cups (500 ml) water
1 chicken stock cube
1 onion
1 tbsp oil
1 tsp paprika
1 can chopped tomatoes
1 potato
2 tbsp tomato puree
1 clove of garlic
Salt and pepper

METHOD

Dice the onion and fry with the crushed garlic in the oil. Add the paprika, followed by the water, stock cube, lentils and then the tomatoes.

Bring to the boil. Season and simmer for 15 minutes. While this is cooking, peel and dice the potato and add after the first 15 minutes. Then simmer for a further 10 to 15 minutes or until potato is cooked.

Season with tomato puree, salt and pepper.

New potato salad

Utensils
Bowl

INGREDIENTS (2 portions)

5 boiled new potatoes
1 small onion
1 tbsp olive oil
½ tbsp red wine vinegar
Chives
Rocket salad or
lamb's lettuche

METHOD
Slice the potatoes, peel and slice the onion
into rings. Mix oil and vinegar and pour the
vinaigrette over the potatoes and onions.
Add the leaves and finely chopped chives.

Bill and Diane Staggs' hire out this
lovely late Westy in California.
Check out this bus and more at
www.vwsurfari.com.

Scandinavian fish soup

Utensils

Large pan

INGREDIENTS (2 portions)

1 small onion

1 carrot

2 potatoes

1 tbsp olive oil

1 ½ tbsp concentrated fish stock

2 cups (500 ml) water

½ cup (100 ml) crème fraiche

1 tbsp tomato puree

10 g saffron

Approximately 15 cherry tomatoes

250 g fillets of fish of your taste
(salmon, cod, hake and plaice work well)

METHOD

Chop the onion. Peel and thinly slice the carrot and potatoes. Fry the onion, carrot, and potatoes in olive oil for a couple of minutes.

Add fish stock and water. Bring to the boil and let it simmer for approximately 10 minutes. Add the crème fraiche, tomato puree and saffron. Simmer for another couple of minutes and season. Split the cherry tomatoes in half and add to the soup. Cut the fish into 1-inch cubes and add to the soup.

Simmer carefully for approximately 5-6 minutes. Serve with a nice piece of crusty bread and butter.

Roberts Westfalia pictured here driving through Yellow Stone National park, USA.

Tomato and tuna fish salad

INGREDIENTS (2 portions)

2 eggs
2 beef tomatoes
1 onion
1 tin of tuna fish in water
Salt and pepper

DRESSING:

2 tbsp apple cider vinegar
4 tbsp olive oil
Pinch of sugar
Basil

METHOD

The dressing: Make up in advance and bottle in miniature bottle. Hard boil the egg. Slice the tomato and onion. Drain the tuna fish. Place the tomato and onion on a plate.

Break the tuna up and place on top of the tomato and onion. Peel the egg and half, lay on top. Drizzle dressing over the salad and it's ready to eat!

This late baywindow is an
ex radio bus! Now sporting
a custom interior, fresh paint and rolling on BRM's!

Tuscany beansoup

INGREDIENTS (2 portions)

1 tbsp olive oil
1 clove of garlic
1 small onion
1 small carrot
1 stick of celery
1 can of chopped tomatoes
2 cups (500 ml) of water

1 vegetable or chicken stock cube
1 can of mixed beans borlotti, canellini etc
1 tsp of fresh or dried rosemary
1 tsp of oregano

METHOD

Rinse and drain the beans. Chop the onion, carrot and celery into small pieces. Crush the garlic and add to the oil in a pan, heat up and before burning the garlic add the vegetables and sweat for a few minutes constantly stirring to avoid burning. Add more oil if needed, once softened pour in the water and stock a little at a time so as to prevent the temperature from dropping to much. Add the tomatoes, beans and the herbs, bring to a simmer and season.

Simmer on a low heat with a lid on for at least an hour, slow cooked over a fire for two plus hours for best results.

Serve with some foccacia or tuscan bread.

(An added bonus if you can get it is some fresh spinach leaves, just roughly chop them and add to the soup a few minutes before serving.)

Curry chicken salad

Utensils

Large pan
Bowl

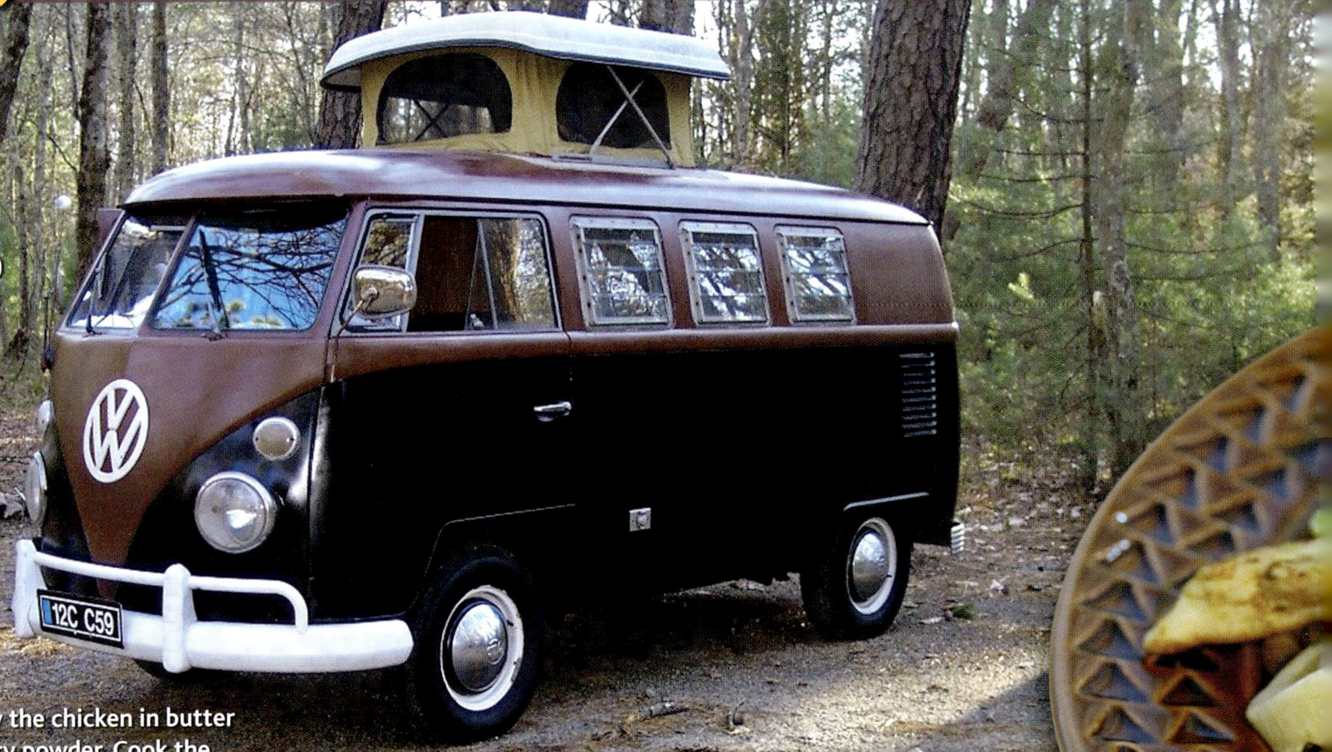

INGREDIENTS (2 portions)

1 chicken breast
Mixed leaves
1 egg
curry powder
Pasta

DRESSING:

Mayonnaise
Curry powder

METHOD

Hard boil the egg. Fry the chicken in butter and a little bit of curry powder. Cook the pasta, drain and cool. To make the dressing mix curry powder with mayonnaise, add hot water to loosen. Mix all the ingredients (except the egg) together in a bowl and add the dressing. Toss and serve! Garnish with egg quarters and serve with pita bread.

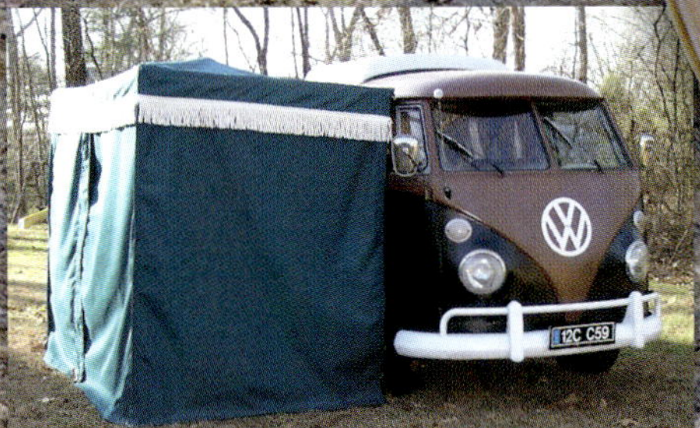

Father and son regulary go camping in the Pachaug state forest, Connecticut (USA) in their '67 Westfalia.

31

Light bites

*These recipes are easy to make –
some can be rustled up quickly
and others will take a spell longer.*

BLT sandwich

Kent Karlsson's 1966 split. Was found in the woods as a wreck and after three years of welding he could finally take the family out camping.

INGREDIENTS (2 portions)

4 rashers of bacon
1 tomato
Lettuce
3 large slices of bread
Mayonnaise
Butter portion
Black pepper

METHOD
Fry the bacon in the frying pan until crispy. Slice the tomatoes. Shred a couple of lettuce leaves. Butter the bread and layer away adding the mayonnaise and black pepper. Ready to eat.

KW 410

Griddle scones

Utensils
Bowl
Frying pan

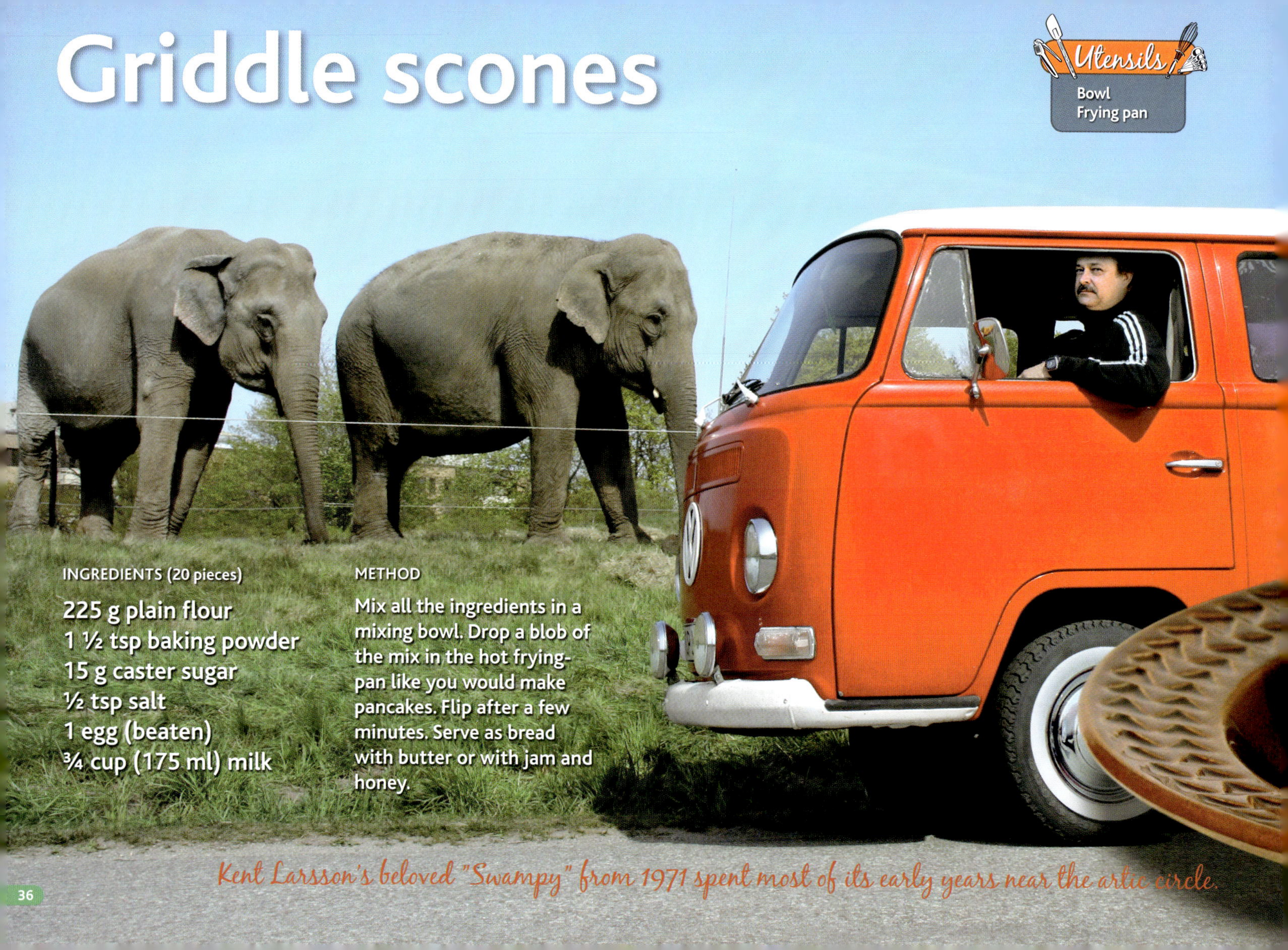

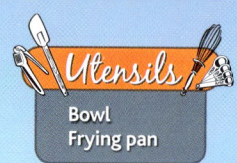

INGREDIENTS (20 pieces)

225 g plain flour
1 ½ tsp baking powder
15 g caster sugar
½ tsp salt
1 egg (beaten)
¾ cup (175 ml) milk

METHOD

Mix all the ingredients in a mixing bowl. Drop a blob of the mix in the hot frying-pan like you would make pancakes. Flip after a few minutes. Serve as bread with butter or with jam and honey.

Kent Larsson's beloved "Swampy" from 1971 spent most of its early years near the artic circle.

Cheese sandwich with bacon and pear

INGREDIENTS (2 portions)

4 large sliced bread
4 rashers of back bacon
1 pear
Cheddar cheese
Butter

METHOD

Cook the bacon until crispy and set aside. Butter the bread on all sides. Slice the pear and the cheese and then layer the ingredients on the bread sandwiching the pear in the middle of the cheese.

Fry the sandwich on a low heat on each side until golden brown.

Darryl Williams' Westfalia in beautiful Nova Scotia, Canada.

Volkskagen sandwich

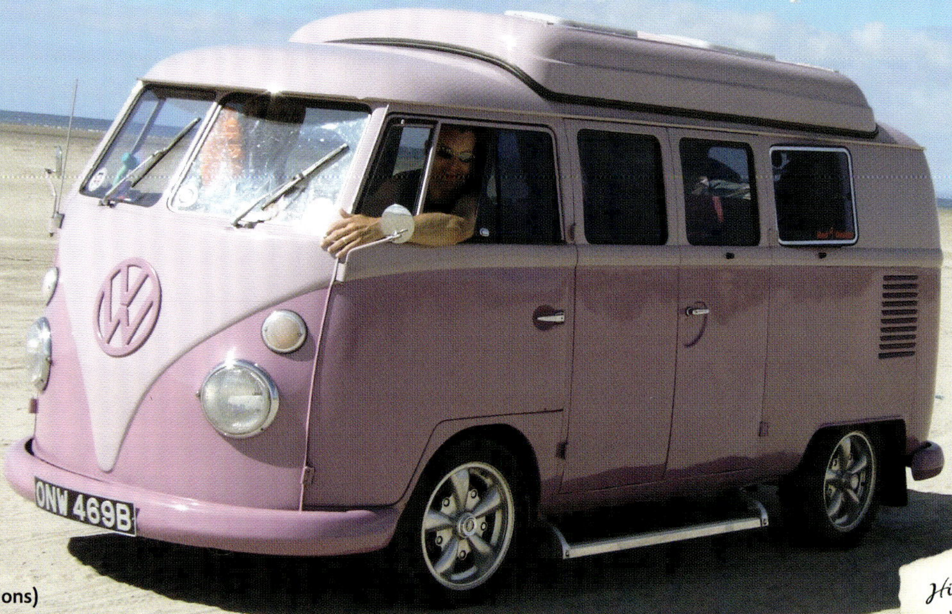

INGREDIENTS (2 portions)

Bread of your choice
100 g peeled cooked
prawns and/or crabsticks
Mayonnaise
Dill

METHOD
Chop the prawns and crabsticks. Mix with mayonnaise and dill. Fill your sandwich. That's it!!

Hi!
We're having the greatest time here in the sun with our '64 Dormobile split at the beach!
–See ya!
Alex van der Arend

ee
ands
les, UK

Smoked salmon with creamy avocado

INGREDIENTS (2 portions)

6 tortillas
6-8 thin slices (approx 200g)
of smoked sliced salmon
2 avocados
Small pot of natural yoghurt
Fresh dill (optional)
A few rocket leaves
Lemon juice
Salt and pepper

METHOD

Skin the avocados and slice lengthways.
Squeeze over some lemon juice.

heat up the tortillas in a dry frying pan
for a minute to soften and then spread
some yoghurt over. Lay a few slices of
salmon, avocado, a few rocket leaves,
(fresh dill), season and wrap up.

Bryan Axell's 1977 Westfalia

Sausage bruschetta

Utensils
Frying pan

INGREDIENTS (2 portions)

4 sausages
1 small onion
½ tbsp mustard
½ tbsp clear honey
Salt and pepper
Butter/oil
French stick or ciabatta

METHOD

Slice the onion and set aside. Now fry the sausages in a little oil for around 10 to 15 minutes until brown and firm. Wrap them in a piece of tin foil and set them aside keeping them hot. Now fry the onion in a little butter/oil until golden brown.

Meanwhile toast or fry your bread. Remove the onions from the pan and add the honey and mustard to the warm pan. Add the sausages back, coating them in the honey mustard. Serve on the bread and top with the onions.

Mike, Kate and Josephines '66 unique head turning split.

KYV 48D

Quesadillas

INGREDIENTS (2 portions)

4 tortilla bread
1/2 cup of grated cheese
6 to 8 cocktail tomatoes
2 pineapple rings
1 green pepper
a few spinach leaves
a good pinch of taco spice
salt and pepper

Utensils
Frying pan

METHOD

Take the tortilla bread and lay one on the frying pan, then sprinkle on a 1/4 of the cheese, leaving a little room at the edge (it will spread when melting).

Slice and dice the tomatoes, green pepper, pineapple and spinach and sprinkle over the cheese, then shake on the taco spice, sprinkle on some on the other 1/4 of cheese and top with the tortilla bread.

Then gently heat over a low heat, turning once. The quesadilla is ready when the cheese has melted and the bread has started colour.

Slice into triangles and serve with guacamole page 134 and salsa page 138. Then repeat!

VW California T5 from Campervantastic – check out www.campervantastic.com where you can hire these fine campers and explore Great Britain in style.

CAMPERVANTASTIC

Tip:
Wrap the Quisidila in greese proof paper and heat the same way to save on washing up the frying pan.

Mains

The ideal campervan cuisine, truly delicious, and a breeze to make anywhere.

Chicken and tarragon pesto pasta

INGREDIENTS (2 portions)

200 g penne pasta
3 tbsp olive oil
2 cooked chicken breasts
50 g rocket salad
Salt and pepper.

Tarragon pesto:
50 g parmesan cheese
50 g toasted pine nuts
Large bunch of fresh tarragon, chopped
Juice of a lemon
1 clove of garlic, crushed
5 tbsp olive oil.

Make the tarragon pesto in advance at home.
Blitz all the ingredients together.

METHOD

Bring a pan of salted water to the boil and add the pasta.
Stir and cook for around 10 minutes. Drain the pasta and
refresh in cold water, then drain once again and toss in the
olive oil.

Grate the parmesan cheese. Toast the pine nuts. Chop
the tarragon. Crush the garlic clove. Mix the parmesan,
pine nuts, tarragon, garlic, juice of lemon and olive oil
together. Your pesto is done!

Place the pasta and the pesto, the chicken and the
rocket in a bowl and toss well. Season with salt and
pepper. Serve straight after.

Utensils

Large pan
Bowl

Ed Skellett's 1958 slammed split panel.

51

Carbonara

INGREDIENTS (2 portions)

4 rashers of smoked back bacon
Spaghetti
1 cup (250 ml) double cream
Parmesan or other **strong**
grated cheese
Salt and pepper
Optional: 1 egg

METHOD
Cook the spaghetti in boiling
water for approx 8 minutes. While
the spaghetti is cooking chop the
bacon into small pieces and shallow
fry over a medium heat for a few
minutes. Add the double cream to
the bacon and bring to a simmer.
Lower the heat and wait for the
pasta. Drain the pasta and add the
cream/bacon mix to the saucepan.
Add the cheese, stir together and
season to taste. Serve immediately.

Optional: Add a raw egg yolk to the
top of the served pasta.

Utensils
Frying pan
Sauce pan

A true classic and it happens to suit th

52

...ervan chef perfectly, as you only need two hobs and two pans and it can be made in fewer than twenty minutes!

Chili con carne

INGREDIENTS (2 portions)

200 g of minced meat
1 onion
¼ cup (50 ml) water
1 tin of chopped
tomatoes

1 clove of garlic
Pinch of salt
2 tsp chili powder
½ tsp oregano
1 small red pepper

1 small tin of baked beans
1 small tin of kidney beans
1 small tin of sweet corn
A knob of butter or a dash of oil

Serve with bread, nachos, rice or a mixed leaf salad.
Nice with a dollop of sour cream.

1 thick bottom
sauce pan

METHOD

Peel and chop the onion. Put the fat in
the pan let it get hot and add the minced
meat. Stir for about a minute and add
the onion. Fry until brown. Add water,
tomatoes, crushed garlic, salt and spices.
Let simmer under a lid for approximately
15-20 minutes. Stirring occasionally.

Split and clear the pepper out of
seeds. Chop into bite size pieces. Add the
pepper, corn and the beans and cook for
another 5 minutes. Season to taste.

Chicken à la King

INGREDIENTS (2 portions)

1 cup (250 ml) sliced meat
from a cooked chicken
1 small tin of mushrooms
OR 100 g sliced fresh mushrooms
1 tbsp butter or oil
1 ½ tbsp flour
¾ cup (175 ml) water (plus possibly
the liquid from the tinned mushrooms)
¼ cup (50 ml) cream
½ cube of chicken stock
1 small red or green pepper
¼ cup (50 ml) of sherry (optional)
Soya sauce
Pepper

METHOD
Put the mushrooms in a deep frying pan. Fry and let most of the liquid evaporate before you add the fat. Let the mushrooms fry for approximately 5-10 minutes. Sprinkle the flour and stir. Add the water, possibly the liquid from the tinned mushrooms and the cream.

Add crumbled stock cube and let simmer for 3-5 minutes. Split, de-seed and chop the pepper. Add the meat and the pepper to the sauce. Bring to heat. Season with pepper, soya sauce and sherry. Sherry is an optional ingredient, but one that makes all the difference!

Serve with rice and a mixed leaf salad.

Corned beef hash

INGREDIENTS (2 portions)

1 tin of corned beef
1 can of boiled potatoes
1 onion
2 eggs
Flat leaf parsley (alternatively dried parsley)
Salt and pepper
Vegetable oil

METHOD

Dice the block of corned beef, potatoes and onion into small 1 cm dice. Heat the pan, add some oil and fry the onion until softened. Then add the potatoes and fry until they start to brown. Next add the corned beef and turn the heat down low. Fry, shake and stir. Add a little of the parsley. Meanwhile get the fried eggs cooking. When the eggs are cooked, turn off the heat, divide the corn beef hash to the plates and top with the fried eggs and serve. Season and sprinkle freshly chopped flat leaf parsley (optional).

Kenneth Johansson's blue 1969 Baywindow.

Ham and cheese omelette

Utensils

Bowl
Frying pan

INGREDIENTS (2 portions)

6 eggs
¾ cup (175 ml) milk
100 g sliced ham
50 g grated cheese
Salt and pepper
Oil/butter

METHOD
Mix the eggs and the milk in a bowl.
Add salt and pepper to taste. Heat the
pan with the oil or butter. Add the egg
mix to the pan. Stir around the edges
with a wooden spoon. When the mix
starts to become firm, put the ham
and cheese on a line along the middle
of the omelette. Fold the omelette
onto a plate. Serve with a green leaf
salad.

1959 23 window deluxe chicken samba.

Chicken chasseur

INGREDIENTS (2 portions)

25 g butter
Half a chicken cut in pieces
3 shallots
50 g button mushrooms
1 ½ tbsp white wine
½ cup (125ml) gravy

1 small tin (200g) of chopped tomatoes
Chopped parsley and tarragon
Salt and pepper

METHOD

Melt the butter in a pan and add the chicken and season. Cook to golden brown all over and then add chopped shallots followed by the wine and cook for 2 minutes. Add the mushrooms, tomatoes and the gravy. Cook on a medium heat with a lid on for approx 30 minutes or until chicken is cooked through. Just before serving stir in the herbs.

Jonny's Swedish 23 window samba, double door, this bus didn't always have so many windows!

Goat's cheese and basil risotto

INGREDIENTS (2 portions)

1 ½ cup (300 g) arborio rice
1 ½ cup (350 ml) water
50 g of goat's cheese
25 g butter
1 cube of vegetable stock
Basil

METHOD

In the first pan, boil the water and add the vegetable stock. In the second pan, melt the butter. Add the rice, basil and start stirring. Keep the heat high and work fast. It is very important to keep stirring the whole time to avoid burning. Add the stock with the ladle a little at a time. The rice will talk to you so listen to it! I. e. it should be making a sound all through the cooking process (sscchhh). Continue to stir until the risotto is cooked (10-15 min).

   When the risotto is ready it should be nice and creamy and have just a tiny little bite to it. Turn the heat off. Break the goat's cheese up and stir it in gently. Add seasoning to taste. Serve with a salad and bread.

VW surfari can hire you this lovely original late Westfalia camper to tour all over sunny California.

Flaming beef Stroganoff

INGREDIENTS (2 portions)

350 g beef fillet (cut into
French fries size strips)
40 g butter
2 tbsp paprika
1 onion
200 g button mushrooms
Vegetable oil
1 ½ cups (350ml) double
cream or sour cream
Dash of lemon juice
Parsley
Salt and pepper
Brandy

METHOD

Melt the butter in the pan and slowly
cook the onion and the paprika until soft
and sweet.

Add the sliced mushrooms and
continue frying for a few more minutes.
Now remove from the heat and place this
mix into the bowl and keep warm.

Place the pan back on the stove and turn
up the heat, add a couple of teaspoons of
oil and when really hot add the steak to
the pan, quickly fry for around a minute
turning the steak and season as it cooks.

Now add the onion and mushroom
mix to the steak and pour in the cream.
Bring to the boil and cook for just a
further minute. Add the parsley and dash
of lemon.

Ready to eat! Serve with rice.

66

This ex fire van comes from the Danish Team Angora Racing Crew.

Chicken fajitas

Utensils
Frying pan

Traditional or with beer marinade – what do you prefer?!

INGREDIENTS (2 portions)

2 chicken fillets
4 tortilla wraps

FAJITA TRADITIONAL SPICES:

1 ½ tbsp cumin powder
1 ½ tbsp coriander powder
1 ½ tsp chili powder
Fresh coriander

FILLING:

1 red pepper
1 onion
Guacamole *(page 134)*
Sour cream
Salsa *(page 138)*

METHOD

For traditional fajitas slice the peppers and onions and chicken into strips. Finely chop the fresh chilli. Sweat the red pepper and chilli in a drop of oil, sprinkle with the spices and then after a few mins turn up the heat and add the chicken and a drop more oil. Quickly cook whilst turning and tossing, 3 to 4 mins. Once cooked, scatter with the fresh coriander leaves.

Make a wrap with the chicken/pepper mix and add the following: Guacamole, sour cream and salsa. Season and dress with a little olive oil.

BEER MARINADE VARIANT:

Try a twist of this recipe by marinating the raw chicken in this beer-marinade:

1 cup (250 ml) dark Mexican beer
2 tsp sesame oil
1 tsp finely chopped garlic
1 tsp dried oregano
1 tsp salt
½ tsp ground black pepper
¼ tsp cayenne

Miguel Alcazar Sanches from Mexico loves his split, regulary travelling in it with his wife.

Fast wok noodles

INGREDIENTS (2 portions)

1 chicken breast
4 nests of noodles
2 small peppers
3 spring onions
1 clove of garlic
1 tsp ginger
1 tsp chili
1 tsp garam masala
4 tbsp oil

METHOD

Place the noodles in a bowl and boil enough water to cover the noodles completely. Add the garam masala, stir in, put a lid on and set aside.

Next chop the garlic, spring onion and the chicken into small pieces and begin to fry it all in half of the oil. After a few minutes of cooking add the spices, the sliced peppers and the remaining oil if needed. Keep stir frying until cooked. Drain the noodles and add to the frying pan. Stir it all around and serve.

You can add cashew nuts and sweet and sour sauce (page 132).

Klaus Springer from Germany own this 1979 piece of art painted by his daughter and her friends on her 10th birthday.

Orange pork chops

INGREDIENTS (2 portions)

2 pork chops or
250 g pork fillet in slices
Butter or oil
½ tsp salt

SAUCE:

1 cup (250 ml) single cream
½ tbsp flour
½ stock cube for meat
½ tsp rosemary
½ tsp soya sauce
Squeezed juice from 1 orange
1 orange

METHOD

Whisk the cream, flour, stock cube, rosemary, soya sauce and orange juice in a sauce-pan. Bring to the boil and let simmer whilst stirring for 3 minutes. Peel the orange and cut into dices. Fry the pork with the fat (pork chops need 3 minutes on each side in a frying-pan). Salt and pepper. Lay the pork and the pieces of orange into the sauce. Bring to the boil.

The dish will look nice if you garnish it with orange peels. Serve with potatoes and vegetables.

Utensils

Large pan
Frying pan

Ian Blake owns this lovely 1965 Canterbury pit conversion splitty.

73

Penne courgette and parmesan

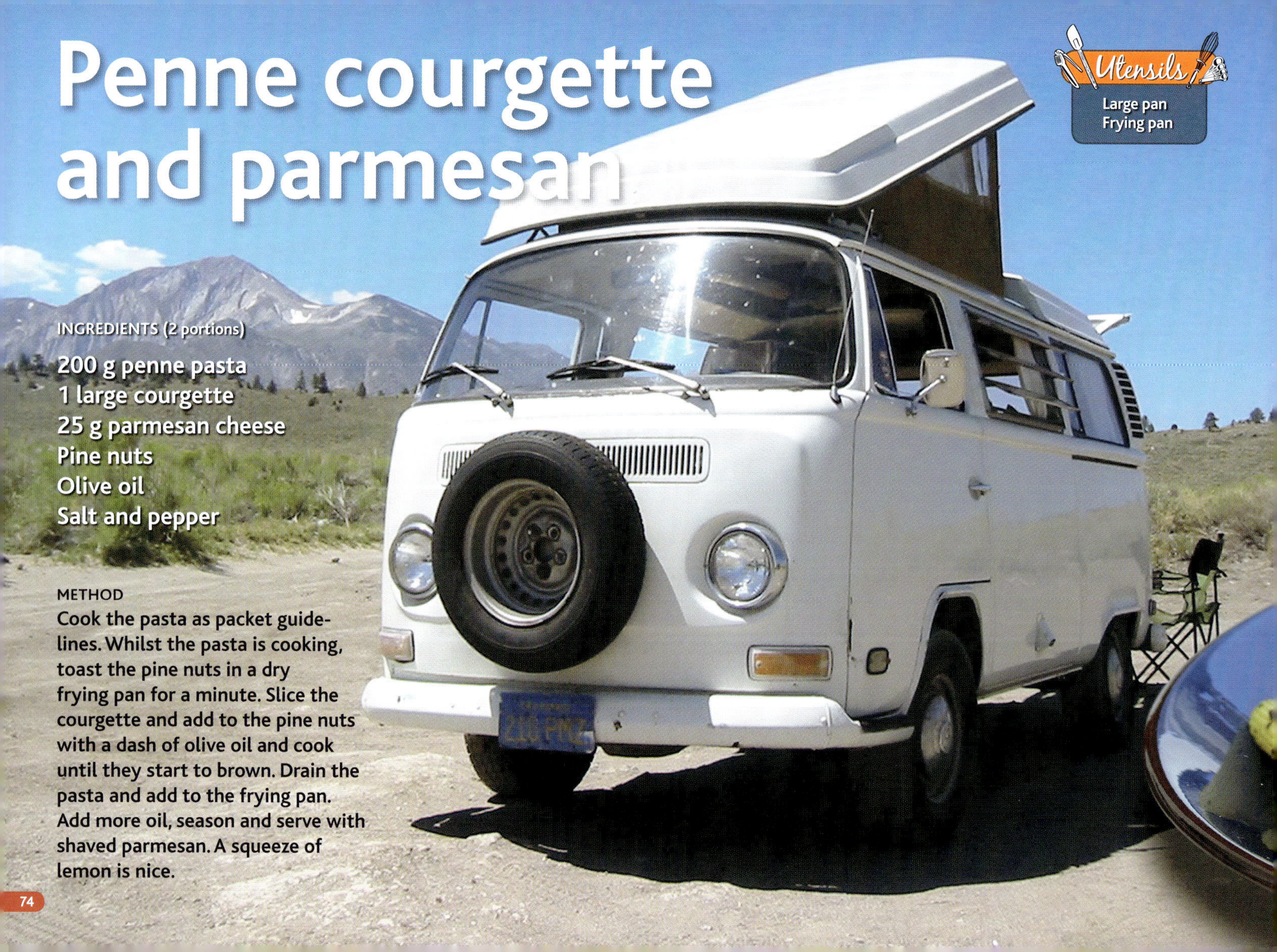

Utensils
Large pan
Frying pan

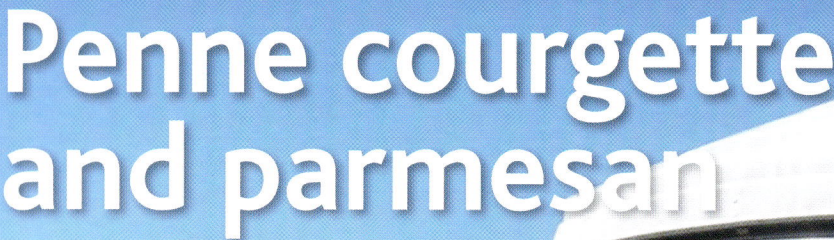

INGREDIENTS (2 portions)

- 200 g penne pasta
- 1 large courgette
- 25 g parmesan cheese
- Pine nuts
- Olive oil
- Salt and pepper

METHOD

Cook the pasta as packet guidelines. Whilst the pasta is cooking, toast the pine nuts in a dry frying pan for a minute. Slice the courgette and add to the pine nuts with a dash of olive oil and cook until they start to brown. Drain the pasta and add to the frying pan. Add more oil, season and serve with shaved parmesan. A squeeze of lemon is nice.

Hans' 1972 Westfalia camping in Sierra Nevada, Mammoth Springs area, USA.

Hotdogstrog

Utensils

Large pan
Frying pan

INGREDIENTS (2 portions)

1 can of hotdog sausages
1 tin of sweet corn
1 onion
1 cup (250 ml) of double cream
1 tbsp tomato purée
Ketchup
Salt and pepper
+ Spaghetti

METHOD

Boil the water. While the water is heating up, dice the sausages and chop the onion. Once the water is boiling, start cooking the pasta. Sweat the onions in the second pan. Once softened add the diced sausages. Fry for approx 2 minutes. Add the drained sweet corn to the onions and hotdogs followed by the cream. Stir the tomato puree into the cream followed by tomato ketchup (for sweetness). Season with salt and pepper until the taste is how you like it. Let it simmer until the pasta is ready.
Serve with the pasta.

Snowtop splitscreen camper. Snowtops were originally built by Freedom Camper, California.

Tagliatelle bolognese

Steve Rocha's 1976 Westfalia travelling across the US. Here in Fruita, California.

INGREDIENTS (2 portions)

200 g minced meat
1 onion
1 clove of garlic
2 tsp dried oregano
1 cube of beef stock
½ cup (125 ml) water

1 tin (400 ml) chopped tomatoes/ 1 jar of tomato sauce
1 tbsp tomato puree
2 tbsp ketchup
½ tsp sugar
Salt and pepper

METHOD

Chop the onion and fry with the minced meat. Fry until brown. Boil the water and let the stock cube dissolve. Add to the mince and bring to the boil. Simmer until almost all the water has evaporated. Add crushed garlic clove and oregano, tomatoes, puree, ketchup and sugar. Simmer for minimum 30 minutes to achieve maximum taste. Season with salt and pepper. Serve with freshly cooked tagliatelle.

Full English breakfast

Utensils
Frying pan/Grill
Small pan

INGREDIENTS (2 portions)

4 rashers of bacon
2 sausages
2 eggs
1 beef tomato
100 g fresh mushrooms
Butter or oil
Salt and pepper
1 tin of baked beans
2 large slices of bread

METHOD

Start cooking the sausages as they take the longest to cook. Cook them under the grill (if you have one), otherwise in a frying pan on a low heat 10-15 minutes. If you want the sausages to cook faster, cut them lengthways which will half the cooking time. Whilst the sausages are cooking, prepare the rest. Quarter the mushrooms. Split the beef tomato in two. Open the can of beans.

Heat the baked beans in the saucepan. Place the bacon and tomato halves next to the sausages. The bacon needs approximately 1.5 minutes on each side, tomato roughly 3 minutes. Fry the mushrooms in fat for a few minutes. Season with salt and pepper. Place the mushrooms on one side of the frying-pan. Fry the two eggs on the other side.

If you are getting cramped for space and some things are cooked, just wrap them up in tinfoil and keep close to the cooker to keep them warm.

Plate the food (don't forget the bread) and get stuck in!

Paul Medhurst famous linde bus
www.type2detectives.com

Spanish tortilla

INGREDIENTS (2 portions)

5 eggs
1 potato
2 onions
1 red pepper
1 small clove of garlic
½ cup (125 ml) olive oil
Thyme
Salt and pepper
Spinach (optional)

METHOD
Peel and slice the potatoes and onion. Split, de-seed and slice the pepper. Finely chop the garlic and thyme. Beat the eggs in a mixing bowl. Place the onions and potatoes into a deep frying-pan with the thyme, garlic and some seasoning. Cover with oil. Cook on medium heat for about 15-20 minutes or until the potatoes are tender. Drain the olive oil and allow the potato mix to cool slightly. Add the eggs to the mix together with the pepper (and spinach) and return to the pan. Cook over a very low heat until the tortilla has set. Serve with rocket and a sprinkle of parsley.

Brian Stoddart can't stay away from the VW scene - here's his precious 1972 Devon Moonraker.

Filling seafood

Fish and seafood make for great cooking and eating when your camping in your van. It cooks quickly, is easy to prepare, and if you're holidaying near the coast then you must check out the fresh fish on sale in the local area.

Mussel's marinière

INGREDIENTS (2 portions)

1 kg mussels
25 g butter
2 shallots, finely chopped
1 clove of garlic
1 cup (250 ml) dry white wine
Fresh parsley chopped
¾ cup (175 ml) double cream

METHOD

Wash the mussels in cold water, removing the beard and scrape the shell clean. Discard any mussels which remain open when tapped or that appear damaged. Using a large pan with a lid, cook the mussels over a medium heat and add a few drops of water to help create a steamy environment for them to cook in. Stir occasionally and once you see the mussels start to open take of the heat.

Remove the mussels from the pan and cover to keep them hot. Place the pan back on the heat and add the chopped shallots and garlic and shallow fry in the butter. Once softened add the wine and stir. Once boiling, add the cream and turn up the heat to get the cream to boil. As soon as it is to the boil, taste and season with salt and white pepper. Remove from the heat and add the fresh parsley. Place the mussels back into the sauce, stir the mussels in the sauce and serve with a lot of crusty white bread.

Break some bread to dip and get
those last drops of sauce!

Pasta sauce with prawns and mustard

Utensils
Frying pan

INGREDIENTS (2 portions)

1 small onion
½ tbsp butter or oil
1 cup (250 ml) crème fraiche
1 tbsp English mustard
½ tbsp Dijon mustard
2 tbsp finely chopped dill
(fresh or dried)
200 g peeled prawns
Salt

METHOD

Fry the onion in the fat without turning brown. Add crème fraiche and bring to boil. Add the mustard and dill. Add the prawns and heat up in the sauce. Season with salt. Serve with pasta, broccoli and freshly ground black pepper.

Jim Merrin's turbo samba on holiday in France.

Thai salmon in coconut sauce

INGREDIENTS (2 portions)

2 shallots
100 g swede
1 carrot
1 small yellow pepper
1 tsp freshly grated ginger
¼ tsp green curry paste
1 tin (400 ml) coconut milk

¼ tsp salt
1 small clove of garlic
1 tbsp fish sauce
200 g fillet of fish
(e.g. salmon)
2 tbsp chopped
coriander or parsley

METHOD

Start with preparing the vegetables. Peel and cut the shallots quarter lengthways. Dice the suede into chunky pieces. Slice the carrots. Dice the pepper into small pieces. Mix the curry paste and approx ¼ cup (100 ml) of the coconut milk in a sauce-pan. Add the rest of the coconut milk, the vegetables, salt, crushed garlic and fish sauce. Let it simmer with no lid for approximately 15 minutes. Dice the fish into inch size (3cm x 3cm) pieces. Place carefully into the casserole and let simmer until cooked, approximately 5 minutes. Season with curry paste, salt or fish sauce to taste. Garnish with coriander or parsley.

VW T4 Model – perfect for pan european adventures! Check out www campervantastic.com for more details.

Serve on its own or with rice or noodles.

Foil baked salmon on a bed of swiss chard and carrots

Utensils
Tin foil

INGREDIENTS (2 portions)

2 pieces of salmon
(approximately 160g each)
Swiss chard leaves
1 carrot
A few sprigs of fresh dill
Butter

METHOD

Butter the foil. Slice the swiss chard and place on the tinfoil. Lay the pieces of salmon on top of the swiss chard. Season with salt and pepper. Slice the carrots lengthways (French fries size) and lay on top of the salmon. Finish by adding a sprig of dill and close the parcel. Make sure it can not leak.

Lay the parcel on the bbq (not too hot) for approximately 20 minutes. Open one parcel after 15 minutes and check how the fish is doing.

Serve with a new potato salad (*recipe page 22*).

Erik Clark's 1966 Westfalia hardtop camping on the Baja Peninsula in Rosarito, Mexico.

93

Tuna and beans

INGREDIENTS (2 portions)

140 g can of tuna in oil
1 clove of garlic
300 g canned cannelloni beans
1 small red onion or a couple of spring onions
Some fresh basil leaves
Salt and pepper
1 tbsp white wine vinegar (optional)

METHOD

First slice the onion and place in a bowl. Then crush the garlic with the flat of a knife, add a good pinch of salt and then mash into a paste using the tip of the knife. Add the garlic paste and the vinegar if you have it, to the bowl.

Then mix the beans and tuna using some of the oil from the can. Gently toss all the ingredients together and serve with basil leaves and black pepper.

No cooking required!

Smoked salmon in a potato pan

Larry Winther's German delivered '65 SO 42 Westfalia and Montgomery Wards swivel wheel trailer.

INGREDIENTS (2 portions)

2-3 peeled boiled potatoes
1 small onion
½ tbsp butter
2-3 eggs
¾ cup (175 ml) single cream
Salt and pepper
200 g sliced gravad or smoked salmon
1 tbsp chopped dill/chervil
1 tbsp butter

METHOD

Slice the potatoes. Peel and chop the onion. Fry the potatoes and onion in butter in a large non-stick pan. Whisk egg, cream, salt and pepper. Pour the egg mix into the pan and let it settle. Stir a bit so it settles between all the potatoes. Lay the sliced salmon on top and let it cook. Garnish with dill and serve with melted butter.

Plaice and prawn parcels

INGREDIENTS (2 portions)

Approx 200 g or 4 plaice fillets
¼ tsp salt
1 small clove of garlic
100 g peeled prawns
25 g spiced butter (butter mixed
with spices such as salt, oregano,
thyme or cayenne)

METHOD

Season the 4 fillets. Peel and slice the garlic. Place the fillets onto a square of tin foil and top with the garlic and then the prawns. Place the butter on top, then fold the tin foil up and around into a parcel.

Wrap up the tin foil together into a moneybag so nothing leaks out. Set the parcels on a warm grill for approximately 10-15 minutes.

The fish is ready when it has turned firm. Serve with new potatoes.

Alternatively lemon sole and haddock can be used.

Jurgen Secher's mango green splitty

Smoked salmon tagliatelle

Paul and Claire bought "Val", a '65 ambulance, on Valentines day. here you see their freshly restored "Lovebus" ready for their freinds wedding.

INGREDIENTS (2 portions)

125 g smoked salmon
A few sprigs of dill
150 g or 6 nests of tagliatelle
1 lemon
½ cup (150 ml) double cream
Fish stock cube
Salt and pepper

METHOD

Boil a large pan of water for the pasta. When boiling take out approximately 1/4 cup (75 ml) of water and crumble in the fish stock cube in the small pan. Add the tagliatelle into the pan of water and cook as packet guidelines. Add the cream and the juice from the lemon to the pan with fish stock. Heat up and bring to the boil. Stir, season and let it reduce a little. Slice the smoked salmon into strips.

Drain the cooked pasta. Remove the sauce from the heat. Add the salmon to the sauce followed by the pasta. Stir. Add dill and serve!

BBQ

Lip-smacking, finger-licking good barbeque recipes. Try wood chips such as hickory or apple in your barbie for some really nice smoky flavours.

Barbeque grilled Mediterranean vegetables

INGREDIENTS (2 portions)

1 large courgette
2 peppers
1 aubergine
1 red onion
Oregano
Basil
Olive oil

METHOD

Cut all the vegetables into pieces large enough that they don't fall through the grate of your bbq or use skewers. Then take all the chopped vegetables and place them in a zip lock bag. Add the oil, some salt and pepper and the herbs. Shake around and leave in the bag until ready to grill.

Grill on the bbq and turn them until char grilled on both sides, then they are ready. You can place them in tin foil and seal them in a parcel and they will keep warm for when the rest of the food is ready.

Funky chicken

Utensils

Charcoal-BBQ
with lid,
Gloves
Tongs

INGREDIENTS (2 portions)

1 chicken
1 can of beer
Salt and pepper
Oil or barbeque marinade

METHOD

Rub seasoning all over the chickens skin. You can also rub on some oil or a marinade. Next open your favorite can of beer and place it in the cavity of the bird, open side up! On a charcoal barbeque sit the bird not over but near the hot coals on the rack, balancing the beer can with the chicken standing up. Close the top of the grill and leave the vent a little open.

Let the chicken roast away for at least an hour and a half. Carefully remove the browned and well cooked chicken from the grill, gloves are a real help here. You will find that the meat falls of the bone!

You can flavour the chicken with smoked chillies or Chipotle paste.

Andy Joiner's black & white 1966 split.
Found in a scrapyard and saved!

Stuffed mushrooms

INGREDIENTS (2 portions)

4 large flat mushrooms
or 8 cup mushrooms
Squeezy cheese in a tube
Chilli spice

METHOD
Clean the mushrooms of any
soil, then pull out the stalks
and discard.

Squeeze the cheese into the
cup or flat of the mushrooms
and then grill on a bbq or under
a grill for a few minuets.

This is one fast and tasty
side dish. Chopped chillies are
a nice touch too if you have
them, but paprika is good if you
don't have the fresh chillies
around.

Chunky stuffed peppers

Utensils
Frying pan
Tongs

INGREDIENTS (2 portions)

2 large red peppers
1 small onion
50 g blue cheese
50 g mushrooms
50 g spinach (fresh or defrosted from frozen)
Salt and pepper

METHOD
Cut the top of the peppers – keep the top for later. Dice the onion and slice the mushrooms. Mix with the spinach, blue cheese and fry the whole lot in a frying pan for a few minutes and season. Now using tongs grill the peppers on all sides. Stuff the mixture into the pepper, place the pepper on top and wrap in foil. Cook on the grill for a further 5-10 minutes.

Lars Secher's rare 1962 double door Samba in sealing wax red and beige grey.

The surfin' is sweet in California!
Rent this bus at www.vwsurfari.com and try
it for yourself…

Grilled halloumi with delicious honey

INGREDIENTS (2 portions)

100 g halloumi
Honey
Herbs
Salt and pepper

METHOD
Slice the halloumi into thick slices
(you don't want it falling through the
grate). Grill on both sides for a couple
of minutes, or until it hardens a bit.
Drizzle with honey, season and add
any herbs you might have. Done!

Full metal jacket

INGREDIENTS (2 portions)

2 jacket potatoes
2 sausages

METHOD

Take the corer and core a tube in the potato. Now take a sausage and cut the tip and squeeze out the sausage meet into the hole in the jacket potato. Pack it in and then wrap the spud in tin foil. Place it on the embers of your fire and wait for an hour. Let cool for a few minutes before eating.

This is a World War 2 rationing recipe!
That's why you find it paired up with
this gun metal grey double door
panel van, owned by Chris Rooker.

Skewered chicken Mexicana

Utensils
Skewers
Zip lock bags

INGREDIENTS (2 portions)

2 chicken breasts
1 small courgette
1 small onion
1 small red pepper
A few cherry tomatoes

MARINADE:

1 tbsp olive oil
½ tsp ground cumin
1 tbsp chopped fresh coriander
1 lime juiced
½ fresh finely chopped chilli
Salt and pepper

METHOD

Soak the skewers in water. Cut the chicken into small cubes. In the bag mix olive oil, cumin, coriander, lime juice, chilli, salt and pepper. Mix and add the chicken. Seal the zip bag and put it in your cool bag for minimum an hour. This stage can also be prepared at home. Slice the courgette, onion and red pepper in fairly big pieces. Thread the chicken, courgettes, onion, pepper and tomatoes onto skewers. Brush the grill with oil and cook the skewers until chicken is cooked through. Turn the skewers so they cook evenly.

Westfalia model T3 also known as the T25 in the U.K. In the U.S.A. and Canada it is called Vanagon. These models where built between 1979 and 1992.

WESTFALIA

DIESEL

SAN DIEGO
CALIFORNIA

OREGON
41574

117

Kofta kebab

INGREDIENTS (2 portions)

200 g minced lamb
1 small clove of garlic minced
½ tsp salt
¼ tsp sambal oelek
½ tsp ground cumin
¼ cup (50 ml) milk

METHOD

Presoak the skewers in water. Mix in a bowl the minced meat, garlic, salt, sambal oelek, cumin and milk. Mould the mixture around 4 skewers. Grill for approximately 8 minutes. Turn whilst cooking. Serve with cous-cous and tsatsiki. *(page 136)*

Honey pistachio chicken

Utensils

Tin foil

INGREDIENTS (2 portions)

2 chicken breasts
5 tbsp honey
25 g pistachio nuts
Salt and pepper

METHOD
Shell the nuts and give them a rough chop. Butterfly the chicken breast by cutting into the thickest side and cut almost all the way through folding it out to look like a butterfly. This will allow faster and more even cooking. Season and grill the chicken on each side until nearly cooked through. Drizzle over the honey and scatter the pistachios on top. Grill a little longer until cooked.

Serve with coleslaw *(page 139)*.

Martin Fothergill's 1959 23 window Samba from Austria.

Todays special on the barbeque menu

Hawaii burger

INGREDIENTS (2 portions)

2 burgers
4 rashers of bacon
2 slices of cheese
1 sliced tomato
Shredded lettuce
1 small tin of pineapple rings
Chilli
2 Seeded baps
Ketchup
Mayonnaise
Tomato/pineapple salsa *(page 138)*

METHOD
Grill the burgers on the bbq. When the burgers are almost cooked, grill the bacon. Toast the buns on the grill for a few seconds. Build the burger and enjoy! ...and don't forget the sauces!

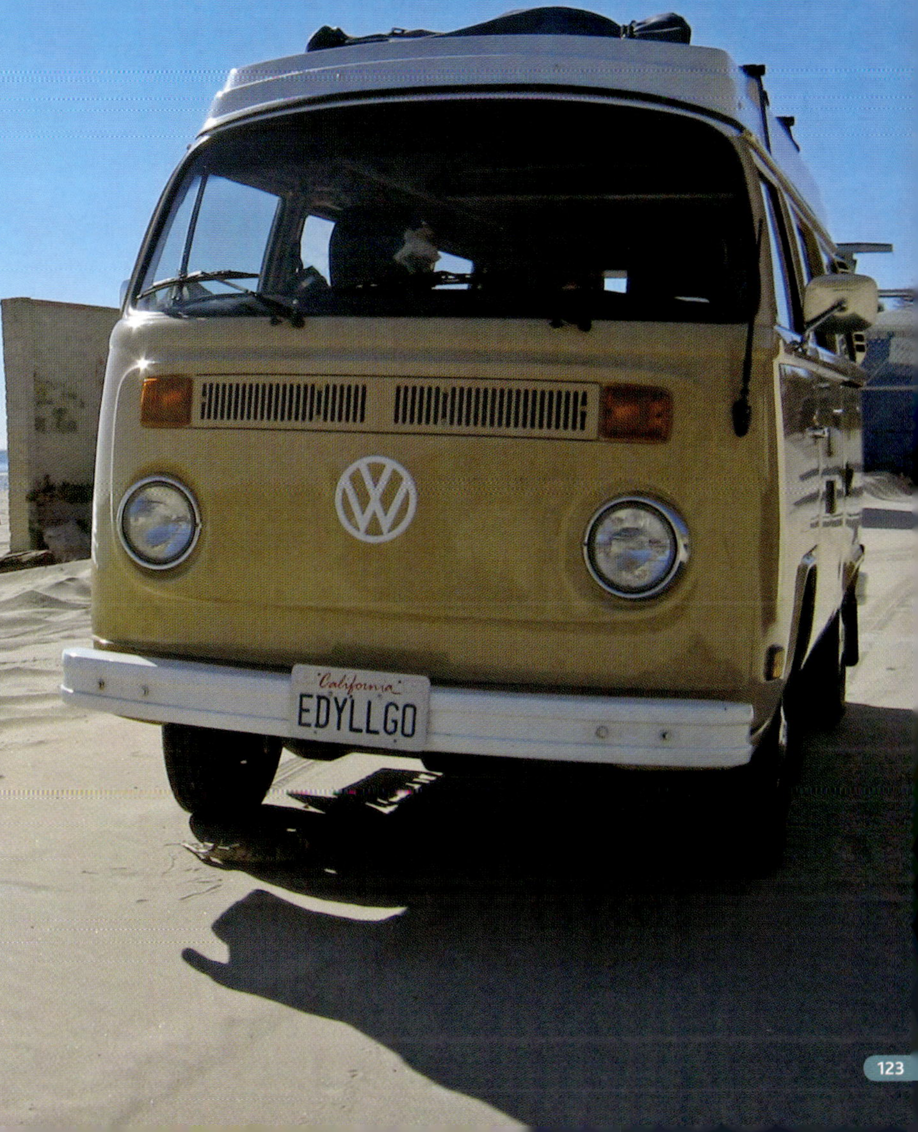

Malaysian barbeque ribs

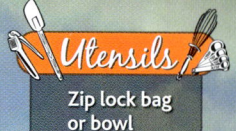
INGREDIENTS (2 portions)

1-2 slabs of pork back ribs

MARINADE:

5 tbsp dark mushroom medium thick soya sauce
2 tbsp oyster sauce
½ cup (100 ml) of brown or white sugar
1 tsp pepper (black or white)
2 tbsp sesame oil
Pinch of salt

METHOD
Place the pork in the bowl or sealed plastic bag and pour over the soya sauce. Then use your hands to coat the pork in the sauce. Next add the rest of the ingredients and mix around coating the pork. Fridge and leave to marinade for at least a few hours.

Steve Garzia, Malta, has this cool 1969 VW kombi and belongs to the club "Daz Maltese Kruisers".

Pork chops with Stilton and cherry tomatoes

Utensils

Frying pan

INGREDIENTS (2 portions)

2 large pork chops
2 thick slices of Stilton
Cherry tomatoes
Salt and pepper

METHOD

This is really easy. Season the chops and grill/fry on both sides until cooked through. Top each chop with the Stilton cheese and top that with halved cherry tomatoes. Cook until the Stilton melts. Serve with jackets, mash or a salad.

Shane Rae's 1971 Westfalia.

Spicy lime grilled prawns

Skewers

INGREDIENTS (2 portions)

8 large tiger prawns
3 limes
2-3 chilli peppers
2 cloves of garlic
Small piece of fresh root ginger
1 small onion

METHOD

Squeeze the lime juice into a ziplock-bag along with all the finely chopped ingredients. Peel and clean the prawns and then add them to the marinade. Do this at least 2 hours before cooking for best results. Thread the prawns onto skewers. Cook over the bbq or under a grill turning once or twice until opaque.

Stuffed mackerel

INGREDIENTS (2 portions)

**2 whole mackerels
125 g (1/2 cup) of almonds
Fresh herbs, these all work well - dill, parsley, chervil, basil, oregano, coriander
Lemon**

METHOD

Cut a slit into the belly of the fish and remove the guts if not already prepared. Then clean the fish with running water inside and out. Next season the fish. Keep it rustic; chop the onion and almonds and slice the lemon into large slices. Hack the herbs a little and then stuff the whole lot into the belly of the fish. Squeeze some lemon juice over and wrap the whole lot in the tin foil. Seal it up and bake it over the BBQ or cook in the embers of a fire.

After around 10 to 15 minutes it's time to peel back the foil and check the fish is cooked through.

Utensils
Tin foil

The lowmilage 1968 Baywindow "Fry".
More info see www.fanofthevan.com

Warm BBQ sauce

Sweet sour sauce

Warm BBQ sauce

INGREDIENTS (2 portions)

1 onion
2 garlic cloves
1 tbsp butter
½ tin (200 g) of chopped tomatoes
1 cup (250 ml) crème fraiche
1 tsp paprika
1 tsp chilli powder
¾ tsp salt

UTENSILS

Bowl
Small pan

METHOD

Peel and chop the onion and garlic and fry them with the spices in the butter. Pour off the liquid from the chopped tomatoes. Add the tomatoes, crème fraiche and salt. Let it simmer for a couple of minutes. Serve the sauce warm to bbq meat or chicken.

Sweet sour sauce

INGREDIENTS (2 portions)

½ cup (100 ml) orange juice (or orange/pineapple)
¼ cup (50 ml) vinegar
3 tsp tomato puree
3 tbsp ketchup
2 tsp sugar
Dash of oil

UTENSILS

Small pan

METHOD

Mix all ingredients. Bring to the boil and let simmer for 3 minutes. Ready to serve.

Tikka barbeque marinade

BBQ beef marinade

Tikka barbeque marinade

INGREDIENTS (2 portions)

250 ml (1 cup) of yoghurt
½ tsp chili powder
2 tbsp garam masala
¼ tsp turmeric
2 tsp ground cumin
2 tsp ground coriander
2 tbsp tomato puree
2 tbsp lemon or lime juice

UTENSILS

Bowl or sealed bag

METHOD

Mix all the ingredients together. Use on chicken breast, drumsticks or wings. Make sure you cut into the meat so the marinade can really penetrate the meat. Coat the meat and leave in a fridge for an hour or two.

BBQ beef marinade

INGREDIENTS (2 portions)

3 tbsp oil
1 tsp lemon juice
1 tbsp soya sauce
1 tsp honey
Herbs of your choice
Salt and pepper

UTENSILS

Two plastic bags

METHOD

Make the marinade by mixing all the ingredients in double plastic bags. Drop the steaks in the bag and squash around. Marinade for at least two hours.

Guacamole

Campervan salad dressing

INGREDIENTS (2 portions)

1-2 avocados
Lime juice
Salt and pepper

UTENSILS

Bowl or sealed bag

METHOD

Mash everything together with a fork or with your hands in a sealed bag.
-That's it!
Once you have tried the original guacamole you can experiment and make your own versions of this classic South American food. Try adding: chillies, garlic, black pepper, coriander or finely chopped onion.

INGREDIENTS (2 portions)

6 tbsp olive oil
4 tbsp balsamic vinegar
1 tsp dried oregano
Salt and pepper to taste

UTENSILS

Small bowl
Whisk

METHOD

Whisk the ingredients together, taste and adjust the seasoning. Pour into a small bottle to store.

Italian tomato sauce

INGREDIENTS (2 portions)

3 tbsp olive oil
I onion
1 garlic clove
1 can of chopped
tomatoes
50 g tomato puree
¼ cup (50 ml) water
½ tsp basil
½ tsp oregano
1 tsp sugar
1 tsp of vinegar

UTENSILS

Small pan

METHOD

Chop the onion finely and crush the garlic into a paste. Add to the olive oil and fry for a few minutes until softened. Add the vinegar and sugar, stir and then add the rest of the ingredients. Stir and mix them around while it heats up. Place a lid on the pan, simmer for 20 minutes on a medium heat.

Beetroot salad

INGREDIENTS (2 portions)

4 small spring
beetroots
Mayonnaise

UTENSILS

Small pan
Bowl

METHOD

Cook the beetroots until soft, around 30 minutes depending on size. Chop the beetroots in small pieces. Place in mixing bowl and add mayonnaise. Stir and serve!

Blue cheese dressing

Tsatsiki

Blue cheese dressing

INGREDIENTS (2 portions)

¼ cup (50 ml) mayonnaise
¼ cup (50 ml) sour cream
50 g blue cheese
1 clove of garlic
1-2 tbsp milk
½ tsp Worcestershire sauce
A pinch of black pepper
Salt

UTENSILS

Bowl

METHOD

Mash the garlic and crumble the cheese. Mix all the ingredients in a small mixing bowl. Let rest for approximately 15 minutes before serving.

Tsatsiki

INGREDIENTS (2 portions)

½ cup (125 ml) Greek yogurt
1 cucumber
2 cloves of garlic
Salt and pepper

UTENSILS

Grater
Bowl

METHOD

Grate the whole cucumber. Squeeze out as much water of it as possible. Put approximately a tablespoon of salt on it and squeeze it again (the salt helps bringing the water out). Place the grated cucumber in a mixing bowl. Add the yogurt and crushed garlic. Season with salt and pepper. Nice to be served with grilled meat or to be used as a dip.

Sour-cream dip

INGREDIENTS (2 portions)

½ cup of sour cream
1 tbsp lemon juice
½ tsp chilli powder
½ tsp ground
coriander
½ tsp ground cumin

UTENSILS
Bowl

METHOD
Mix all the ingredients
together.

Sweet sour-cream dip

INGREDIENTS (2 portions)

½ cup or sour cream
1 tsp of honey
1 tsp ground
cinnamon

UTENSILS
Bowl

METHOD
Can be used as a dip or
dressing for fruit and
salads.

Tomato salsa with a twist of pineapple

Peanut sauce

Tomato salsa with a twist of pineapple

INGREDIENTS (2 portions)

1 tin (400 g) of chopped tomatoes
1 small tin of pineapple
1 fresh chilli
1 tbsp tomato puree
1 clove of garlic
1 tsp sugar
Salt and pepper

UTENSILS

Bowl

METHOD

Drain the chopped tomatoes. Mix with the tomato puree. Finely chop the chillies and crush the garlic. Add the chillies, garlic and sugar to the tomato mix. Season with salt and pepper. Dice the pineapple in small pieces and add to the salsa. Done!

Peanut sauce

INGREDIENTS (2 portions)

1 can of coconut milk
½ cup crunchy peanut butter
1 fresh chilli

UTENSILS

Small pan

METHOD

Chop the chilli finely. Then add all the ingredients to a pan. Bring to a boil and stir for a few minutes. Serve warm or cold.

Coleslaw

INGREDIENTS (2 portions)

1 large onion
2 carrots
¼ small white cabbage
Salt and pepper
Mayonnaise

UTENSILS

Bowl
Grater

METHOD

Grate the carrots. Slice the onion and cabbage. Season and mix in the mayonnaise until evenly covered.

Sweets

According to archaeologists they now
have undisputable proof of a higher
civilisation before us. Their vehicles
had superior style and they could make
a chocolate cake almost anywhere.

Camper chocolate cake

INGREDIENTS (2 portions)

50 g butter
½ cup (125 ml) sugar
¼ cup (75 ml) flour
1 ½ tbsp cacao
Optional: a couple of drops
of vanilla essence
1 egg

METHOD

Choose the largest pan you have with a thick bottom. Melt the butter in the pan. Take it off the heat and add all the ingredients except the egg. Stir. Then add the egg. Make sure the egg doesn't curdle by stirring vigorously. Place the pan back on low heat with a lid on and leave to cook without stirring for approximately 10 minutes. Check the cake after 5 minutes to check it isn't burning. The cake is done when it is spongy in the middle and sticky on top. Serve with squirty or pouring cream.

Paul's 1958 Westfalia came with many rare camping extras such as propane fridge, floor furnish and a toilet.

Baked bananas

INGREDIENTS (2 portions)

2 bananas
Marshmallows
Chocolate
(dark chocolate works best)

METHOD
Leaving the skin on, cut a "V" shaped channel into the top (inner part of curve) of the banana and remove flesh. Replace the slice of flesh with marshmallows and chocolate so that the banana is stuffed. Wrap with tin foil and place in coals of campfire or on the BBQ. Roast each side for about 5 minutes. Remove with tongs. Peel foil back. Enjoy!

Try different sorts of chocolate bars and find your favourite taste. Good ones to banana are Snickers, Bounty or Toblerone.

145

Pancakes

INGREDIENTS (2 portions)
1 egg
1 cup (250 ml) flour
1 ¾ cups (400 ml) milk
Pinch of salt
Little butter or oil
for frying

Utensils
Frying pan
Bowl

METHOD
Put the egg in the bowl. Add half the amount of the milk. Add flour little at a time whilst whisking. Add the rest of the milk and whisk to a smooth paste with no lumps. Add a pinch of salt and a drop of vegetables oil or melted butter. Now heat up your frying-pan so it is really hot. Melt a knob of butter and pour in enough mix to cover the pan. You may need to swirl it around to cover the surface. Cook for a few minutes or until the surface has dried. Then it is time to turn it over or flip it in the air if you're feeling confident.

Alternative toppings: sugar and lemon, maybe you have some jam portions, cream, chocolate sauce or blue berries.

A 1963 split screen camper from down under.

French toast

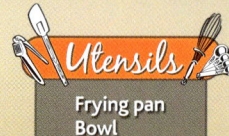
INGREDIENTS (2 portions)

2 eggs
A pinch of salt
½ tsp sugar
½ tsp cinnamon
1 cup (250 ml) milk
6 slices of white bread
Butter or oil

METHOD

Crack the eggs into a bowl. Beat lightly with a fork. Stir in milk, salt, sugar and cinnamon. Put a little oil or butter into the frying-pan and while it is heating up, soak the bread on both sides in the egg mixture for a few seconds. Soak only as many slices as you will be cooking at one time. Cook until golden brown, turn and brown the other side. Make sure it is properly cooked before eating. Serve with fruit yoghurt and fresh berries.

Safaris rule! And so does this '67 pastel blue double door split with matching caravan, owned by Markus and Lotta in Sweden.

Hot cinnamon apples

INGREDIENTS (2 portions)

2 apples
4 tbsp sugar
2 tbsp cinnamon
25 g butter

METHOD

Peel and core the apples and cut into wedges. Melt the butter in a sauce-pan over a medium heat. Add the sugar and cook for a few minutes then add the apples and stir. Cook for a few minutes until softened, you can add a little water if needed. When the apples have softened sprinkle over the cinnamon and serve immediately with a dash of cream.

George Hornington's 1975 Fleetline from South Africa.

"You can freeze the cinnamon apples and take with you in your cooler on your next outing"

Rice pudding

INGREDIENTS (2 portions)

160 g long grain rice
3 cups (700 ml) milk
Juice of a lemon
1 tsp cinnamon

METHOD

Place the rice, milk, cinnamon and lemon juice in a pan and bring to the boil. Lower the heat and simmer for approx 25 minutes. Add a little more milk if required. The rice should be very tender and the liquid absorbed. Can be served with lemon zest or a dollop of jam.

Early standard split screen from Finland.

Campfire popcorn

INGREDIENTS (2 portions)

Some popping corn
1 tsp oil
Season with sugar or salt depending on your taste

METHOD

Using a disposable foil take away dish, the kind you get from the Chinese takeaway. Place a tea spoon of vegetable oil in the dish followed by a layer of popping corn. Fit the lid on and crimp down the edges. Place on your fire/bbq and leave until you have heard all the popcorn pop.

You can speed things up by blowing into the embers of the fire, raising the temperature. Give the dish a shake from time to time and be careful when opening. Season with salt or something sweeter.

This is Phil Dodsworth 1961 split screen samba, imported from Oregon USA. Amazingly he converted it to automatic and switched from left to right hand steering as well as many more custom touches.

Sugared almonds

www.planetmelling.co.uk

1979 moonraker by Devon, owned by John Melling

INGREDIENTS (2 portions)

1 egg white
1 cup blanched almonds
½ cup (125 ml) granulated sugar
1 ½ tsp ground cinnamon
A pinch of salt
1 tbsp butter (melted)

METHOD

In a small bowl beat egg white until frothy. Add almonds; coat completely. Drain excess egg white from almonds and set aside.

In another bowl, mix sugar, cinnamon and salt. Add drained almonds and coat completely.

Place nuts in a disposable foil take away dish in a single layer. Place pan in the centre of cooking grate. Cook 14-16 minutes, turning nuts once halfway through grilling time. When your nuts turn a dark brown, brush with butter to coat completely. Let cool before serving.

White hot chocolate

INGREDIENTS (2 portions)

¾ cup white baking chocolate,
chopped or grated
3 cups (750 ml) milk
1 tsp cinnamon
1 tbsp vanilla
Whipped cream

METHOD
Heat the milk, cinnamon and white
chocolate in a sauce pan until the
chocolate melts. Add vanilla. Serve with
whipped cream on top. Lovely!

Perfect for that cold lovely winterday trip!

Make your own gingerbread bus

Utensils
Rolling-pin
Oven

INGREDIENTS

1 1/2 cup (300 ml) sugar
1 cup (250 ml) light or dark syrup
100 g butter
1 tbsp ground cinnamon
1 tbsp ground ginger
1 tbsp ground cloves
1 1/2 cup (300 ml) milk
1 tbsp bicarbonate
Approximately 1 kg flour

METHOD

Mix sugar, syrup and butter in a sauce-pan. Heat until the fat has melted. Then add the spices and milk and put aside to cool. Mix the flour with the bicarbonate in a bowl. Add the cold butter with spices and milk to the bowl and mix to a nice firm dough. Wrap it in plastic film and keep in the fridge over night.

Putting it together: Melt some suger to caramel in a frying-pan. Let it go into a nice light brown colour – don't burn it, watch it closely. Dip parts in the melted suger and put together fast. Look out! Watch your fingers, this gets really hot and sticks to your skin like napalm.

Decorate with icing sugar, candy and whatever you like. We've been using liquorice for tires and smarties on top.

Draw the parts on paper. You can download templates from vwcampercookbook.com

Pre-heat the oven to 175 degrees. Work and roll out the dough with some flour on a table to a nice 2-3 mm thickness.

Lay the templates on the dough and cut out the parts.

Bake in the oven – smaller parts 5-7 min. Bigger parts between 10-15 min.

More tips on www.vwcampercookbook.com

Index